Narad

Inner Journey

Inner Journey
Copyright : Prisma, Auroville
Author : Narad

First edition 2023

ISBN 978-93-95460-66-8 (Paperpack)
ISBN 978-93-95460-78-1 (ebook)

BISAC Code:
POE000000, POETRY / General
POE009000, POETRY / Asian / General
POE003000, POETRY / Subjects & Themes / Inspirational & Religious

Thema Subject Category:
DC, Poetry
DCF, Poetry by individual poets
D, Biography, Literature and Literary studies
DSC, Literary studies: poetry and poets

Cataloging-in-Publication Data for this title is available from the Library of Congress.

Published by:
PRISMA, an imprint of Digital Media Initiatives
PRISMA, Aurelec/ Prayogshala,
Auroville 605101, Tamil Nadu, India
www.prisma.haus

To Sri Aurobindo, Lord and friend, who has given me so much love and force that my only words are of gratitude and humility.

PREFACE

In this book of poems I have included many of my experiences on the path along with poems to others who have borne the trials and tribulations of rising to a higher life through the Integral Yoga. These are for the most part recent poems in the years 2000 to 2022.

Poetry seems often to spill forth and I must type rapidly to catch the subtleties and nuances that come through. I am grateful to all who have sent me or expressed to me their appreciation of my poetry but as always, I am only a scribe who writes in humble gratitude to Sri Aurobindo for His divine largesse.

Narad

Contents

1. Behind the Heart 9
2. A Child of God 10
3. An Erring Pilot on the Ship of God 11
4. A World of Peace and Calm 12
5. A Presence Growing in the Soul 13
6. Before Time's Done - To Mary Helen 14
7. All Things New 15
8. A Razor's Edge 16
9. Children of Immortality 17
10. A New Day 18
11. A Shining Light 19
12. A Transformed Race 20
13. Arindam Basu 21
14. As His Kin 22
15. Aspiration of a Higher Kind 23
16. Beneath the Surface 24
17. Build in Me 25
18. Dreams of Beauty 26
19. Evolving Soul 27
20. Compassion of the Seer 28
21. Dance and Sing 29
22. Dwell in Eternity 30
23. A Transformed Race 31
24. A World of Peace and Calm 32
25. Our Errant Ways 33

26. Pilgrimage to the East	34
27. The Beloved's Kiss	35
28. The Far Transcendences of Love	36
29. The Light That Falls	37
30. What More Is There to Say	38
31. When Visited by Love	39
32. Will We Hold Out?	40
33. Avatars from Eternity	41
34. Eternal Love and Beauty	42
35. Evolving Man	43
36. Evolving Soul	44
37. Experience Divine Delight	45
38. Fled the Night	46
39. Following Truth	47
40. Forbidden Fruit	48
41. God Is With Us Now	49
42. God Our Full and Final Trust	50
43. God's Vast Design	51
44. Godhead's Gift	52
45. Harmony	53
46. He is in Me	54
47. He Will Hear My OM	55
48. I Bow in Humility	56
49. I Live Alone	57
50. I Rest in Thee	58

Behind the Heart

The years since your departure have swiftly flown
And only the memory of your beauty abides
Together with the love your soul had shown
And the peace within my soul that still survives.
I feel that you have taken birth again
Perhaps a dozen times or even more
To grace the earth and fill the hearts of men
As you did once in ages gone before.
We met and Mother upon you cast Her smile.
I think in solitude of your beauty and grace
That merged with me and filled my life awhile
And held your love that nothing can efface,
Behind the heart, the psychic being's place.

March 13, 2022

A Child of God

There is a soul who is facing a power cult
Who believe they have the authority and right
To decide the fate of one who laboured here.
A child of God choosing to live in light
Is now denied an entry in Auroville.
With demands to her that she bow and agree
To their monitoring her daily work and life,
This soul who has offered herself for twenty years
As a volunteer accepting the work they gave!
Will the ego be abolished in our time
And collective harmony become
The leader of our human destiny?

January 11, 2022

An Erring Pilot on the Ship of God

I am a pilot on the ship of God
Who has lost his compass and cannot find the way.
After years of searching does it not seem odd
That I have foundered in an unknown bay,
Who met the Mother in the time of youth
And found in Her the inner spirit's goal
Yet still am I at eighty-four uncouth
And lacking in the essence of my soul.
The leverage that once it seemed I caught
Is far from me as my errant craft plies on
And a battle rages, one that must be fought
Until is reached the Supramental Sun.

A World of Peace and Calm

You are entering now a world of peace and calm
Where flowers speak in muted tones of love.
Rest here awhile and feel the healing balm
And touch the zephyr as through you it will move
And the brightness of the sun upon your hair
And the lapping water warm upon your feet.
Here is a place most elegant and fair
Where the universe and psychic being meet.
Come stay in this atmosphere of unbridled joy
Allow the force of light to let you in
To a sanctuary where no evil force can toy,
And the healing of your longing soul begin.

A Presence Growing in the Soul

I entered into darkness once again
And felt a pressure build within the heart
And as with all transgressions suffered pain
And must make amends or from this world depart.
There is no sin but there is ignorance
Or willful turning back from the light's ray,
Yet there is no fate or sign of random chance
For all here is delight and all is He.
And yet we stumble and we often fall
Though we are not evil as religion says
And deaf to beauty and the Spirit's call
Or the descent of the transforming rays.
Although we seem at times far from the goal
There is a Presence growing in the soul.

Before Time's Done - To Mary Helen

I walked upon love's path enfolding thee,
A soul that seemed at times too rare a gift
For one as I who lived so vitally,
A child embracing Nature's vast uplift.

But then the heart recalls the joy of days
Among the laughing flowers, kindly trees,
Communicants with Nature in her ways
And moments filled with happiness and ease.

We marveled at the brilliant flare of sky
Appearing as the red sun disappears
Or a lone bird's notes of soulful ecstasy
When all the multi-coloured morning nears.

I'll meet thee once again before time's done,
Thy shining soul illumining my sight
As stars reflect the glory of the sun
And know thee as I've known in life thy light.

All Things New

Golden in the sunlight of Her smile
Aspirants and devotees of light,
Upturned faces opening out the soul
Recipients of bliss in great degrees,
Divine largesse the gift supreme on earth.
Perhaps the legions of the darkness plan
A final thrust before their fated end
Or so appears this sad embattled world
So full of promise despite the wrath of man
Upon his kin, upon his very self,
Denying Grace, abandoning the Dream,
To self-destruct in some predestined hell
Or cling to Truth as sinks the falsehood's night
And the pain and dark necessity of death.
But One has come and shown the sunlit path
And sung of all the glory still to be,
For earth and man shall rise to heaven's heights,
His promise to the deep surrendered soul,
And Love shall touch the offered and the blessed.
Already one can feel the New World close,
It presses lightly on the doors of life
Inviting us to step with faith and joy
Through gossamer curtains of the heart's divide
And look at all things new that are the same
Uncovered of the cloak of ignorance,
Revealed in beauty as the mystic rose.

A Razor's Edge

It is a razor's edge we walk upon
For now the world has grown to satiate
The few who dwell in darkness; light has gone,
Truth into falsehood grown and love to hate.

The Supermind is felt by more than the few
Who call themselves disciples and devotees,
For when the old is dying out the new
Seems distant and falsehood flourishes to please

Those who gravitate towards filth and mire.
Few are they who heed the inner call,
Few who can withstand the cleansing fire,
Yet many know but willingly forestall

Within the truth that has descended here
Perhaps from loneliness, desire or fear.

January 19, 2022

Children of Immortality

We are children of immortality
And must rise into the eternity of Light
Allow the revealing of infinity,
Find the sunlit path, beautiful and bright

And know ourselves beings most divine
Of the one of many names we name as God.
All earthly beauty is but a living sign
And nothing in the universe is odd

Or out of place, for all is only He
And as we grow in consciousness will know
Something of the play of divinity
And understand the path on which we go

To merge with Him and feel divine delight
Arisen from our own self-chosen night.

A New Day

In the company of those who know the way
I feel a subtle presence pressing down
And reading the lines of Savitri I pray
That one day on earth Beauty shall wear her crown

And all the world celebrate in love
And ananda that fills the longing heart,
These earthly heavens high towards which we move
That all may know the Mother's plenary art.

How close we have come to mass destruction and more,
But there are forces that uphold the crown
Promised to man behind the golden door
When first we took birth slowly drifting down

To earth in human bodies built of clay,
From ignorance to rise into new Day!

A Shining Light

Now the sweeping rain upon us comes
Relentless is its grace upon the soil
And thunder with its sound of battle drums
Gives us brief rest from our lifelong toil.

From my window, deeply drawn within
I watch the frolic of the dancing wind
And know there is on earth no lasting sin
But in the aftermath of evil find

A shining light, precursor of our way
And in companionship with regal stars
We move once more towards a lustrous day
Healed of duality's multitudinous scars.

Escorted into light now free of doubt,
The helping hostile forces ushered out!

A Transformed Race

The treacherous roads we must drive in the rain
Are nothing to the roads our spirits face
To cleanse the dirt within again and again
Preparing for the beauty of the race

Steadily descending from above,
Below, within, in every human being
To manifest the truth of selfless love,
Divine that we be granted the light of seeing

And may move toward the hour fixed by God
That we, limited, advancing through the years
Evolving from the worm and from the sod
Done with ego emptied of all fears

May be participants in a world of Grace
And bliss, forerunners of a transformed race.

Arindam Basu

Meeting him was like a galactic fire,
Embraced by him I could not understand
The lessons that he taught me in the night.
I heard the voices of the stellar choir
And the music of a composer named Sunil.
I sang the OM with older Ashramites,
Disciples and devotees who lifted me higher
To heavens where man is not allowed to come.
In Auroville a stellar choir formed
To bring down from eternal heights the songs
That the angelic choirs sing to men.
My music became a prayer to the Divine.
And he the guru who led my soul to Her.
We opened a channel for the Lord's voice to sing
Through us, an instrument harmonious
A united voice of earth before the Lord.

As His Kin

When I alone yet in Her hands secure,
Am hobbled still by the recent past
Living in ignominy, impure,
The words of the once beloved on me cast

A darkness darker than Walpurgis night,
A shadow of the evil drawing near.
And yet there is in me no hint of fright
Or minuscule emotion based on fear.

When we surrender to the Lord our souls
Evil lurks behind a friendly door
And though the love and beauty once known falls
On us, we are not alone, we can adore

The Master of our lives hid deep within
Who knows us as His friend and as His kin.

Aspiration of a Higher Kind

The light is playing softly in the trees,
My dreams of ages past are lying there
Dreams of former lives I could not seize,
Busy with self I had no time to spare.

And now again reborn in Auroville
I work for Her without the ego's rule
Aspiring still my destined role to fill
In the early stages of the spirit's school.

We grow from birth to birth, there is no doubt
But only through sincerity can achieve
The peace that comes so silently and out
Of it we live in Her, we do not grieve

For sin and errors on the long and arduous way
But live in love and all our life we find
The Grace that once seemed lost is here to stay
And aspiration of a higher kind.

Beneath the Surface

I have delved beneath the surface of the sea
And found a world of beauty and surprise.
My aquatic teachers lesson me,
In realms of wonder to my youthful eyes.

Yet more I see, a consciousness supreme,
For One who came into my life is there
Although to shuttered minds the waves might seem
Thunderers demonic without care.

The goggles and the fins, the awkward mask
Allow all souls to dive these sacred fields.
Our lives are set to bear the human task,
To offer self and all as being yields

To the Divine at every unknown turn
That in our hearts the fire may always burn.

July 29, 2022

Build in Me

How great an inner progress one must make
When the beloved's falsehood seems to shake
The pillars of a spiritual unity
That fall with the pain of insincerity.

Protect me Lord from all deceitful lies
And from the arrows of the enemies
Of truth and sanctity in humankind
And the vagaries of doubting mind.

Build in me a citadel of peace
That I might stand free in that eternal hour
When the force of the apocalypse descends
And soul meets soul embracing now as friends.

Dreams of Beauty

When still a child I sang of all my dreams
Of beauty manifest on this troubled earth.
Experiences came to me in golden streams,
Divine in nature, exceeding worldly worth.

Yet old desire to me strongly clings
And anger in moments raises its ugly head,
The errors of my life bear painful stings
And seem the product of a mad instead!

Vainly I try to thwart and overcome
The denizens who would my future steal
My efforts yield a small and paltry sum,
The inner wounds so difficult to heal.

Come now Mother, touch me once again,
Purify me, keep me without stain.

2020

Evolving Soul

The manifold dimensions of a man
Still half animal since thought began
And inner vision peered through weakened eyes
Seeing a golden future to surprise
The intellect which seemed to know it all
Yet could not bear the power of the call
And hid within its whitewashed walls of thought;
And yet in moments of seeing truly caught
The thread of oneness in the vasts of space,
The elementary beginnings of a race
Supreme among the vestiges of men
Who like beasts confined within their pen
Hug their precious lot and their desires
And when the body fails and spirit tires
Give up the soul to realms of peaceful rest
Preparing to return and face the test
Of transformation and the godly goal
The bright renascence of the evolving soul.

March 13, 2022

Compassion of the Seer

The indigence of mental man is clear
He has reached the summit, now locked in a tower
Unable as yet to see the Light or hear

The enlightened voice of the Enlightened Power
Unless he leaps above the realm of thought
And in the silence of the mind attend

To the Word that seekers of the Truth have sought
He may come to an evolutionary end,
For now the gods have come on earth to man
Seeking to uplift his soul and bring him near

To divinity, since human time began
Through the sacrifice and compassion of the seer.

Dance and Sing

Hour by hour the transforming Force descends
Though few on earth of its beauty are aware
It touches some and all this life attends
To a new force approaching, blessing this fair

Yet troubled earth and with infinite care
From heights beyond imagination wends
Its way with Graces in the morning air
And each asuric force its force upends.

Those who clearly are called may live in peace
And progress on this path so filled with light
Where ignorance and impertinence shall cease,
No longer will bewildered Nature fight

And all shall join, to earth the anthems bring
And joyous realized souls shall dance and sing.

Dwell in Eternity

There must be a true surrender
In the mind and heart of man,
No longer can the vital wander
Or attempt to thwart the new world's plan.

If at times there will be a fall
One must rise up from the dust
Attend again the inner call
And all the inner being trust

In the transformation of the race
And from the animal ascend
To divinity and guide
The spirit in us to transcend

This scattered life, this poverty
Of soul and dwell in eternity.

March 13, 2022

A Transformed Race

The treacherous roads we must drive in the rain
Are nothing to the roads our spirits face
To cleanse the dirt within again and again
Preparing for the beauty of the race

Steadily descending from above,
Below, within in every human being
To manifest the truth of selfless love,
Divine, that we be granted the light of seeing

And may move toward the hour fixed by God
That we, limited, advancing through the years
Evolving from the worm and from the sod
Done with ego emptied of all fears

May be participants in a world of Grace
And bliss, forerunners of a transformed race.

A World of Peace and Calm

You are entering now a world of peace and calm
Where flowers speak in muted tones of love.
Rest here awhile and feel the healing balm
And touch the zephyr as through you it will move

And the brightness of the sun upon your hair
And the lapping water warm upon your feet.
Here is a place most elegant and fair
Where the universe and psychic being meet.

Come stay in this atmosphere of unbridled joy
Allow the force of light to let you in
To a sanctuary where no evil force can toy
And the healing of your longing soul begin.

Our Errant Ways

Only the material sheath remains
Blessed raiment of the Godhead's gift,
Symbol of the sacrificial gains
For man endured his spirit to uplift.
In this room of mortal life now dwells,
Enlightening, enrapturing our days
The Presence of the Mother in our cells
Transforming by Her Love our errant ways.

Pilgrimage to the East

We were young and the call of the mysteried East
Ran swiftly through the blood of our youthful veins.
Unknowing the mind was pulled across the earth
By the beckoning spirit's laugh, the invisible reins
Of joy attending the hour and hope of new birth.

Now in the dusk of memory there flee
Fragments of beauty, scent of the mystical rose
Intimations of an arcane mystery
Glimpses of the inner being thrilled
At the spark that in our bosom silently grows
And love refound and life again fulfilled.

The Beloved's Kiss

I meet your children on the evolving way
And meeting them I find I often pray
That you may touch them as you have touched me
With the stamp of your divinity.

How many souls are seeking in the dark
Of mind and self, wishing to embark,
Upon a path that truly they can take
If once the earthly baubles they forsake

And cling to Truth that guides the seeker's way,
Learn to weep in gratitude and pray
For light to come into the dark abyss
And wait in calm for the Beloved's kiss.

January 19, 2022

The Far Transcendences of Love

I've known the wine's extravagance
And found desire in the ways,
Lost the bloom of innocence
In the headlong rapture of my days.

But One who stood at the fiery gate
Encouraged me to boldly go
And seek my path yet consecrate,
Remembering the burning glow

She lit within this room of life,
Awaking the Sleeper from his dreams
Of worlds untenanted by strife,
To launch this craft on sunlit streams

And meet in perfect realms above
The far transcendences of love.

The Light That Falls

When my beloved's face is aglow with love,
Speechless I feel her soul conjoin with mine,
For ours is a sanctioned gift from worlds above
This painful earthly realm our lives confine.

Yet we have held communion with the trees
And flowers known, their secret essence shared,
Marveled at such miracles as these
Two spirits in the net of God ensnared.

Slowly as the days turn into years
We are grown closer still, divinity
Envelops all the hours, a Presence nears
That fills us with divine felicity.

Enfolded by such Grace no sorrow's tear survives
The light that falls on our enamoured lives.

What More Is There to Say

What more is there to say,
Souls in sorrow weep
Shattered hearts replay
The hour of death to keep

Alive the dying face
Beloved of all things.
Remembrance is a grace
To which our being clings

Until we realize
The soul in us that knows
Nothing ever dies,
To life there is no close

And we must carry on,
The need for death explore
Until the work is done
And God is found once more.

When Visited by Love

When we no longer carry ego's shield
Or halberd of our insignificant thought
And see in others enemies to yield
On bloodstained fields in senseless battles fought,

When we no longer need the taste of tears
And open to the wonder of it all,
God from our shadowed background reappears
Responding to the spirit's urgent call.

Then shall we truly wake and realize
The One who in each living creature dwells,
Who looks on us with calm compassionate eyes
As light divine invades our human cells.

The lotus from the mire blooms above,
So too our lives when visited by love.

Will We Hold Out?

Will we hold out against the evil's thrust
Or fall and in a desperate failing chance
Finally accept the offer of the Grace.
Or is sedentary man too satisfied
With his minute kingdom now established here
To take the leap and on the precipice
Walk into the sunlight of Her smile?
I know that all creation moves towards Thee,
The cycles turning upward see Thy Face,
O Mother, the creatrix, guide our steps
And would that we be willingly free.
May that hour dawn O Lord of Peace,
May the evil of this world finally cease.

January 2, 2022

Avatars from Eternity

What evil could they wreak upon me now
Having forced me to delete the sayings of my friend
And wiser brother to whom I gave my vow
To stand by his side until the darkness' end.

What are the words of the devil's minions to me
Who has met the Mother in all humility
And Sri Aurobindo, Lord, whom I did see,
His Presence the gift of eternity.

The days are longer now, the years reduced
And I, time's traveler at last come home
No longer by desire's claims seduced
Or in vagaries of mind induced to roam.

Whatever I must bear I offer to Thee
Accept this child into Thy infinity.

Eternal Love and Beauty

The innocence I lost when I was young
The chants of orthodox choirs that were sung
Come back to me as I alone in pain
Go through the karmic struggles once again.

How little have I grown despite the Grace
That welcomed me in that most sacred place
Where one could work in peace and meditate
Arriving to a contemplative state

Where all seemed beautiful and half divine
In an ashram of a singular design,
To build a race of beings to bring down
The Golden Force, the spiritual Crown,

That all the earth might join to celebrate
The end of desire and greed that only sate
Those who defy the edict of the Divine,
Eternal love and beauty are the sign.

Evolving Man

Now from my secret heart I shall disclose
The friends who willingly brought me to this place
Where peace the gentle silence enfolded those
Great spirits, the burgeoning of a new race,

And those who carried light within their soul
Kin to me in those far ages past
Solemn souls and joyous who heard the call
And knew that evil and falsehood could not last

In the sun of India and its men
Of faith and power, sages most divine
Who come to earth to uplift the world again
Carrying in them the transformative sign

That man evolve to a resplendent height
Suffusing earth with the supernal light.

Evolving Soul

The manifold dimensions of a man
Half animal still since thought began
And inner vision peered through weakened eyes
Seeing a golden future to surprise
The intellect which seemed to know it all
Yet could not bear the power of the call
And hid within its whitewashed walls of thought
And yet in moments of seeing truly caught
The thread of oneness in the vasts of space,
The elementary beginnings of a race
Supreme among the vestiges of men
Who like animals confined within their pen
Hug their precious lot and their desires
And when the body fails and spirit tires
Give up the soul to realms of peaceful rest
Preparing to return to face the test
Of transformation and the godly goal
The bright renascence of the evolving soul.

March 13, 2022

Experience Divine Delight

Will we one day in consciousness perceive
Colours unimagined to the human eye
Distances and time we could not believe
With the human mind's present capacity?

Will we be able to access the higher planes
Of eternal beauty, truth and eternal love,
Reaching the sacred stars, attaining gains
That once lay below or throned above

This human field of constrained narrowness,
Break out into a world of infinite bliss
Touch the One who is all tenderness
And suffer the moment of her transforming kiss?

Will we evolve and with a subtle sight
Experience in life divine delight?

Fled the Night

If I should leave and leaving fail to see
One final time on earth your radiant smile
No regret will I have for there will be
Within my heart a reverential file

Of every moment you kissed this aging head
Or touched with graceful hands this offered face,
Not for an instance will come fear or dread
For in the chamber of this heart your place

Assured in years gone past and those to come
Will be a living remembrance, no, a fact,
That you are with me in my spirit's home
Awaiting in golden silence the next act!

Cherished one, beloved, angel of light
For us there is only dawn, fled the night.

Following Truth

Many I meet in Auroville seem lost
Or busily engaged in personal things
Few speak of Mother and unknowingly are tossed
Upon the waves of ego and it's stings.

There is a complicated bureaucracy
Scattering and dividing each from each,
Where now the beauty of human unity,
The true pranams that seem beyond the reach

Of this community to be built on peace.
Will the internecine quarrels never end,
Will vehemence and anger never cease
Can those in power ever their way amend?

This the city built for unity
And one day truly following truth shall be.

Forbidden Fruit

The taste of the forbidden fruit is sweet
But like the serpent's fangs leads to an end
Of bitterness and the crime of love's deceit
And in the darkness lonely days portend.

And yet the vital ego fulfilling desire
Recks not the cost nor the pangs of grief
Of those who have felt the sacred living fire
Whisked away like the fingers of a thief.

When shall we baring self allow the soul
To lead the pilgrimage and set the path
Surrender to its singular control
Obliterating falsehood and its wrath,

The many faults that we must expiate
And in humility find our sanctioned state.

God Is With Us Now

You are entering now a world of peace and calm
Where flowers speak in muted tones of love
Rest here awhile and feel the healing balm
When Nature choosing from her beauty's trove

Adorns the earth with festive blooms and hues
Bringing to tired eyes the gifts divine
Her living treasures and her transcendent views,
The mathematics of her grand design.

All speak of consciousness but hardly know
The path of progress towards human harmony
Or strive to find the road on which to go
And see the world a hostile dynasty

Nor strive to find the crown or holy grail.`
All mortal efforts seeking unity
Betray us with the mind and we fail
But this is temporal, not destiny,

For God who dwells secure within each heart
Is ever with us and never will depart.

God Our Full and Final Trust

Shall we not rise up and front enclosing night
Of dark and formidable power lust,
Can we not turn again to the transforming light
And put in God our full and final trust?

There seems within our mortal myopic view
A falsehood creeping and a deep despair
In those who felt and aspired for the new
Consciousness with truth and love to pair

With the descent that the avatars, the Two
Have brought to earth, a radiance untold
A vision and a promise for the few
Who take the leap and daring all the cold

And calculating forces that disdain
The advent of the truth that shall remain.

God's Vast Design

We have travelled long upon the ego's road
And what have we achieved in our quest
Necessity and desire our nature's load
Obscured the blessed entry of the Guest.

Governments lie in shambles and deceit,
Conglomerates seek foremost in their greed,
Control of the world, the working masses cheat
And plant in human hearts division's seed.

I live alone, companion to a thought
That constantly recurs within my soul,
Remembering the battles I have fought
Aspiring to reach the ultimate goal,

Union with the Mother, truth divine,
And the Supramental, Godhead's vast design.

Godhead's Gift

The inner Antarctica where lies frozen mind
Incapable to free itself from fear,
A throwback to the world of animal kind
Recipient yet of the knowledge of the seer

And still entombed in desire and deceit
Arrogant and lustful, filled with greed,
Unable to bow humbly before Their feet,
So great this life's accumulated need.

Will common man survive the Light's descent
Or harbour cowering in darkness' lair
Injured psychically, his nature bent
Towards destruction of the true and fair.

There are souls aspiring, hoping to uplift
This race at last, accepting Godhead's gift.

Harmony

I live in peace with one who lives for love,
Not vulgar or in the lust that now we see
But pure like an angelic force above
Descended to earth in stellar harmony.
It is a moment in life's history
When all is cleansed and darkness is no more
And soul is open and can truly see
The light that has broken through the golden door
And all is one, a force of unity.
The hour has come and silently appears
On this whirling earth, so blessed and so fair,
That all the darkness that has reigned these years
Evaporates in jasmine-scented air.

He is in Me

I stood alone before an iron hill
And looked upon the very face of God
Of earthly pain I have had my fill,
But seeing him my little mind felt odd

For why should He be only a mountain top,
If He is everywhere why not in me
And then to thought there came a sudden stop,
Where then is God and what is infinity?

Is there a time when time is not or space
Can I see God in the finiteness of sand,
In the forms or colours of a different race
Or bid him come to me at my command?

No, I experience him in eternity
And find him sweetly in and out of me.

He Will Hear My OM

These poems descend without the aid of thought
As if the Gods were pouring them into me
Falling rapidly only to be caught
In moments when the soul is calm and free:

They often appear full-rhymed or in blank verse
Oft in iambic pentameter they come
When I am shot with pain and grief or worse,
In quatrains of the sonnet's sacred home.

How often have they come when all seemed lost
And death my hidden friend drew very near
His coming not to bless me or accost
My soul or hope to instill in me great fear.

When done is my earthly work for which I came
He will hear my OM as I chant the Mother's name.

I Bow in Humility

I have remembered You in births long past
And will do so in splendours still to come
And in some future life when light is cast
Upon this sleeping soul I will come home.

All that remains for me is eternal You
As I struggle in this world to unite
My soul with You and in surrender view
Not looking up or down but into Light.

Peace I pray You grant this wanting soul
To be Your slave through all the realms of time
One who knows but has not yet attained the goal,
Who sings and prays receiving every rhyme,

Each poem's descent as guide and grace to me,
Your gifts, your love receive with humility.

I Live Alone

I live alone in this constricted space
No longer the place my body knew as home
My needs are few and gone is the usurped place
Of joys and tears that frequently would come,

Unwanted visitors to disturb the inner peace.
Living alone with the Alone yet not alone
These poetic lines from Him do not cease
And the OM resounds in me an eternal tone

Singing the strophes of infinity.
Upon my strings the Lord of the Universe plays
Symphonic are his sounds that enter me
Pulsating and pressing on the world to raise

The level of consciousness, participate
In the arrival of the Gnostic state.

I Rest in Thee

In my heart, O Lord, I would assuage
The wrongs I have done unconsciously,
The moments of my resistance and my rage
For when I sinned I sinned most joyously.

The years have taught some silence and some calm
A realization of the vital nature's stress
Have soothed at times with pure and heavenly balm
The restlessness which Thou hast deigned to bless.

I offer now my soul, my work, my sight
To Thee who hast given incomparable gifts to me
And through this offered body seek the light
And the promise of immortality.

Whether in this life or future lives to come
I rest in thee my psychic being's home.

International Publications

Auroville Architecture
by Franz Fassbender

Auroville Form Style and Design
by Franz Fassbender

Landscapes and Gardens of Auroville
by Franz Fassbender

Inauguration of Auroville
by Franz Fassbender

Auroville in a Nutshell
by Tim Wrey

Death doesn't exist
The Mother on Death, Sri Aurobindo on Rebirth
Compiled by Franz Fassbender

Divine Love
Compiled by Franz Fassbender

Five Dream
by Sri Aurobindo

A Vision
Compiled by Franz Fassbender

Passage to More than India
by Dick Batstone

The Mother on Japan
Compiled by Franz Fassbender

Children of Change: A Spiritual Pilgrimage
by Amrit (Howard Shoji Iriyama)

Memories of Auroville - told by early Aurovilians
by Janet Feran

The Journeying Years
by Dianna Bowler

Auroville Reflected
by Bindu Mohanty

Finding the Psychic Being
by Loretta Shartsis

The Teachings of Flowers
The Life and Work of the Mother of the Sri Aurobindo Ashram
by Loretta Shartsis

The Supramental Transformation
by Loretta Shartsis

**The Mother's Yoga - 1956-1973 (English & French)
Vol. 1, 1956-1967 & Vol. 2, 1968-1973**
by Loretta Shartsis

Antithesis of Yoga
by Jocelyn Janaka

Bougainvilleas PROTECTION
by Narad (Richard Eggenberger), Nilisha Mehta

Crossroad The New Humanity
by Paulette Hadnagy

Die Praxis Des Integralen Yoga
by M. P. Pandit

The Way of the Sunlit Path
by William Sullivan

Wildlife great and small of India's Coromandel
by Tim Wrey

A New Education With A Soul
by Marguerite Smithwhite

Featured Titles

Divine Love

The texts presented in this book are selected from the Mother and Sri Aurobindo.
"Awakened to the meaning of my heart. That to feel love and oneness is to live. And this the magic of our golden change, is all the truth I know or seek, O sage."

Sri Aurobindo, Savitri, Book XII, Epilog

A Vision by the Mother

On 28th May 1958, the Mother recounted a vision she once had of a wonderful Being of Love and Consciousness, emanated from the Supreme Origin and projected directly into the Inconscient so that the creation would gradually awaken to the Supramental Consciousness. The Mother's account of this vision was brought out a first time in November 1906, in the Revue Cosmique, a monthly review published in Paris.

A Dream – Aims and Ideals of Auroville
the Mother on Auroville

50 years of Auroville from 28.02.1968 - 28.02.2018
Today, information about Auroville is abundant. Many people try to make meaning out of Auroville – about its conception, to what direction should we grow towards, and, what are we doing here?
But what was Mother's original Dream and what was her Vision for Auroville back then?

Matrimandir Talks by the Mother

This book presents most of Mother's Matrimandir talks, including how she conceived the idea for this special concentration and meditation building in Auroville.

Memories of Auroville - Told by early Aurovilians

Memories of Auroville is a book about the very early days of Auroville based on interviews made in 1997 with Aurovilians who lived here between 1968 and 1973. The interviews presented in this book are part of a history program for newcomers that I had created with my friend, Philip Melville in 1997. The plan was to divide Auroville's history into different eras and then interview Aurovilians according to their area of knowledge. Our first section would cover the years from 1968 till 1973 when the Mother was still in her physical body.

The Way of the Sunlit Path

May The Way of the Sunlit Path be a convenient guide for activating this ancient truth as a support for a Conscious Evolution.
May it illumine the transformation offered to us in the Integral Yoga.

A Dream Takes Shape (in English, French, Hindi)

A comprehensive brochure on the international township of Auroville in, ranging from its Charter and "Why Auroville?" to the plan of the township, the central Matrimandir, the national pavilions and residences, to working groups, the economy, making visits, how to join, its relationship to the Sri Aurobindo Ashram, and its key role in the future of the world. This brochure endeavours to highlight how The Mother envisioned Auroville from its inception, some of the major achievements realised over the years, and some of the difficulties currently faced in implementing the guidelines which she gave.

Mother on Japan

I had everything to learn in Japan. For four years, from an artistic point of view, I lived from wonder to wonder. And everything in this city, in this country, from beginning to end, gives you the impression of impermanence, of the unexpected, the exceptional... ...everything in this city, in this country, from beginning to end, gives you the impression of impermanence, of the unexpected, the exceptional. You always come to things you did not expect; you want to find them again and they are lost – they have made something else which is equally charming.

Auroville Reflected

On 28 February 1968, on an impoverished plateau on the Coromandel Coast of South India, about 4,000 people from around the world gathered for a most unusual inauguration. Handfuls of soil from the countries of the world were mixed together as a symbol of human unity. Why did Indira Gandhi, the erstwhile Prime Minister of India, support this development for "a city the earth needs?" Why did UNESCO endorse this project? Why does the Dalai Lama continue to be involved in the project? What led anthropologist Margaret Mead to insist that records must be kept of its progress? Why did both historian William Irwin Thompson and United Nations representative Robert Muller note that this social experiment may be a breakthrough for humanity even as critics commented, "it is an impossible dream"?

A House For the Third Millennium
Essays on Matrimandir

Nightwatch at the Matrimandir...
A cosmic spectacle; the black expanse above, the big black crater of Matrimandir's excavation carved deep into the soil. The four pillars - two of which are completed and the other two nearing completion - are four huge ships coming together from the four corners of the earth to meet at this pro propitious spot...

Passage to More than India

This book is a voyage of discovery. In 1959 the author, Dick Batstone, a classically educated bookseller in England, with a Christian background, comes across a life of the great Indian polymath Sri Aurobindo, though a series of apparently fortuitous circumstances. A meeting in Durham, England, leads him to a determination to get to the Sri Aurobindo Ashram in Pondicherry, a former French territory south of Madras.

www.ingramcontent.com/pod-product-compliance
Lightning Source LLC
LaVergne TN
LVHW010434070526
838199LV00066B/6023